Stranger to Blue Water

Voices of West Virginia

a Poetry Anthology

Edited by

Daniel McTaggart

Stranger to Blue Water

Edited by Daniel McTaggart

Associate Editor: James P. Wagner (Ishwa)

For Terry McNemar, one of the funniest storytellers I ever met. You are greatly missed.

Foreword

This past September 2017, I had the great honor of being named state Beat Poet Laureate of West Virginia. It was there I met fellow laureate of NY-Long Island, James Paul Wagner. We talked a bit about parts of New York we'd both been to, but not together, of course. Fast forward a couple of months and James and I are talking about poetry.

He asks what the poetry scene in West Virginia is like. He was curious about the essence of a state nestled in the mountains. West Virginia may not be known for its poetry, but it is for its imagery. John Denver sang about it. Pearl S. Buck is from here.

So there is a lineage.

The people in this book are points on the poetic spectrum of the mountain state. Some are poets of note. Some haven't gotten the notice they deserve. All are part of the consciousness that elevates our culture.

I wanted to show James a variety. I wanted to include poets with words gentle as dust falling through sun, refreshing as whitewater spraying in the face, and solid as the mountains on which we all walk and live.

Like me, I think you'll find yourself dancing to these words. Perhaps listening to sounds unheard of before in silence. This is West Virginia, where voices abound in the air between all the hills and valleys. You want to know what poetry is like in our state? Reading this anthology is your first step.

Enjoy your hike.

~ Daniel McTaggart
West Virginia Beat Poet Laureate 2017 - 2019

Table of Contents

William F. DeVault

Three point two

it took over two hundred stitches
in his face
to close the result of his quest to get more than three point
two beer.
His car going briefly ballistic
off the Point Marion Bridge.
I wonder what stories he tells to his family and friends,
decades later,
when asked about the Universal monster movie scars
that render him self-conscious and somewhat terrifying.
and whether or not
a six pack of Pennsylvania beer
was worth it.

rhododendron hells

the only way to get the small town taste out of your mouth
is to bury it in concrete and neon and artificial turf.
taking pride in accomplishments not accomplished by you
but by transient out of state recruits and a misplaced
burrito.
the same flowers bud and rise and bloom and wither.
there is yet honor in hard work, and when you lie
only to yourself it makes it easier to choke down
prison food.

Arthurdale

Eleanor Roosevelt came to the dedication
subsistence farming for coal miners under the new deal
where the cards were still marked, the decks still stacked,
but the strawberries were a nice touch.
my Uncle Fred, the toughest man I'll ever know,
lived out his life there, taking in strays
and walking row after row of strawberries
to catch the rapacious box turtles plundering his crops.
half the tall tales of DeVault boys of my father's
generation
begin and end with him, someday I'll tell you a few.

Emily

truth be told, it wasn't my first crush but my...
third...
when I fell for the freckle-faced girl at Wiles Hill
Elementary.
the first was Jenny, in kindergarten, ponytails and a
slightly gap-toothed smile.
the second was Susan, the slightly cross-eyed
(or so her glasses made her out to be)
blonde who was too busy worshipping Paul McCartney to
pay me mind.
but Emily struck sparks at 11 and all her quirks made her
irresistible.
It was an epically doomed and star-crossed love,
chaste to the point of ridiculousness (not even a kiss)
but the conversations
we had behind the school at recess made my brain do
somersaults.
and when I saw her at my senior prom, more than half
a decade later,
on the arm of my bitter rival from the Wiles Hill
playground,
I had to smile. For memory and unconsummated dreams.

My grandmother's lost teenage years

there's a hole in time between when she worked as a
domestic
and when she met my grandfather, thirty-five years
her senior,
at the county fair. she never spoke of those times,
and there were no telling artifacts to dwell upon.
just the awareness that something hardened her.
put an edge on her tongue and a coil in her spine
that made her ready to fight anyone and anything.
the marriage was short and tempestuous.
two kids, one who nearly died from polio (my mother).
curses and threats. she never took a penny from him
in child support.
she didn't want to be beholden to him.
probably there are those who know the truths, as ancient
as they are,
as I know legacies and legends from her and other's lives
that I am sworn to keep secret. locked away like the ring
I found in her jewelry box.
ten karat gold and stone long gone. not unlike a heart
hollowed out.
filled with her children and grandchildren, but still
something.
something she never explained. perhaps it is best.
perhaps.

William F. DeVault, the current reigning US National Beat Poet, counts Morgantown, West Virginia as part of the pastiche of his life. His parents came from the area, and he spent many years there, graduating from Morgantown High School in 1973. It was there in Morgantown some of his most memorable early works were written, including *The Unicorns, Monument*, and *dance of the decades*. He is the author of more than twenty books of poetry, and in 1996 was named the Romantic Poet of the Internet by Yahoo!

Scott Emerson

Visiting Grandpap

I rap my knuckles against the door
politely
so I don't startle him
but he already knows
I'm there
he's got a monitor
set up in the living room
to catch cars
entering the driveway

I wanted to wait for my
sister
he knows her car
he also lives alone
and he's got a gun
and strangers
make him uncomfortable

The curtain in the window
peels back revealing
a wedge of
wizened face, jowled,

one green eye
still bright
suspicious

And who might
you be?

Your grandson.

I say it loud
Pap's hearing is bad
and the door is
thick

Who?

It's Scott.

There's a pause
It's been a long time
since I came here
a decade and a half
of petty familial bullshit
he can't remember
and that I try to forget
until his 92-year-old brain
catches up, reconciles

my name with the unfamiliar
face at his doorstep

Kristen's brother?

That's me

Slowly the door opens
and I ease over the
threshold
careful not to move too
suddenly

Just so you know
he says
I'm prepared
in case you're
wrong

Blue Horizon Drive-In,
October 21, 1992

the speaker posts left behind
stand in the dying light, uniform rows
throwing black-cross shadows

over them rises the screen
a great weathered headstone
awaiting an epigraph

Voices

The neighbors are on their back porch
again
disembodied in fresh darkness
talking about nothing much
in loud monkeyhouse whoops

they like the word *fuck*
but don't know how to use it

their conversation sailing on night's breath
into my room, making itself
at home, making it hard
to write

I already carry too many voices
inside my skull, thoughts
demanding to transmogrify
into something tangible, useful
something I can send into the world
like an SOS shoved in a bottle

or a letter of protest nailed to the
neighbor's sagging screen door
asking them to please
shut the fuck up

She Dragged Me Here & I Loved It

I

She dragged me here
to this filthy men's room stall
shoving her tongue into my mouth
by way of introduction
before
lifting her leather skirt--
her smooth pale pubic mound
wet, musky--
relentlessly riding me
battering the head of my cock
with her cervix
screaming, coming
biting my earlobe hard
enough to draw blood

&
I loved it

II

She dragged me here
to another friend's party
shallow vapid people
waving socially-conscious microbrews
with the right amount of ironic detachment
avoiding me yet again
as I wait in the corner
anticipating another bout
of makeup sex
until I finally make eye contact
with her--
standing between two polo-shirted fucks
deigning to acknowledge me--
before
rolling her eyes in disgust
and leaving
with somebody else

&
I barely feel it this time

III

She dragged me here
to this raw, gaping hole
in the earth
ignoring my pleas
my promises to change
as I pounded on her box--
the lid's underside leaving
splinters deep inside my hands,
blood from the final
blow she gave me
still welling in my eye--
before
dumping me
punctuating her bitter laugh
with a shovelful of
dirt

&
I find it very hard to breathe

Poem
9/15/2015

Standing in the presence
of gods we tremble
not, raising cracked clay
faces toward the darkening sky
in joyous defiance
unencumbered by eternity
the burdens of the infinite
so many grains of sand sifting
through our fingers

How we laughed at the great
immortals, at the weary gait
with which they dragged themselves
across millennia, their ceaseless
disappointment in our human flailings,
their impotent thunder in the face
of our impudence

We mocked
their envy, their seething resentment
of our deaths, for despite the vast
wealth of strength and power, the
bottomless font of their wisdom,

the gods will forever exist, tired hands
wrenching the cogs of time ever
forward, not once knowing
the release of decay
yearning for the freedom we find
as molecules
floating
in a lungful of dust

Scott Emerson's work has recently appeared in *Year's Best Hardcore Horror Vol. 1, Horror Sleaze Trash, Quick Shivers About Bugs, Destroy All Robots!,* and *Diner Stories: Off the Menu.* From 2010-2016 he served as facilitator for Morgantown Poets, a not-for-profit group that hosted free literary events. Dividing his time between WV and PA, he's currently working on a number of literary projects he's not allowed to talk about.

Erin Geil

28 Days Without Running Water

June was hot and late in the month
it comes in bits and pieces, how I try to forget it,
the chunks of time, and the moment I screamed
at the ceiling, at the house, as though it could even
hear my insanity. First there was no word,
and then they said they'd fix our water leak
in October, but it was now late July and hotter.
It fried your skin like chicken, that outside air.
October, October, and then it'd be over.
But you need running water. You need it to bathe,
you need it to shower; you need it for cleaning,
for boiling. You need it to live, but they sat and did
nothing. And after 28 days we grew desperate
as a family in the U.S. of A. Two elderly parents,
and me the daughter, denied running water.

Rode Them Like Highways

Bare me,
the flesh
skin shakes
the core
of what
the world
saw
the day it
turned its
head away
and glimpsed
the crumb
sitting
in that
poor girl's
worked
hands.
Lines
you couldn't
see,
covered
in their
own wasted
filth

of
thoughts
for you that
didn't move
more than
the
rats
did,
as they
journeyed
across
the ones
that still
lived,
but were
too broken
to scream
them away;
the rodents
rode
them
like highways.

Alfe-betik

Across balconies,
connected destroyed,
erected from groundlings
here in jurisdiction.
Killing lemmings,
murdering nonsense,
oppressive pockets.
Quiet rumblings
sauntering toward
unannounced vagrants.
Withstand xenophobia
you zephyr.

Limbo of Us

Waiting for words
Of something
Meaning more
There is weight
To my breath
Holding me
Down inside, an
Anchor
Plummeting
To a place
Never touched.
The way his
Fingers moved
Into my hand,
Marking me,
But not with
His scent, or his
Body, but with
His spirit.
A spiritual marking.
Waiting for words
To quiet the stirring
Of the shadows
That pass through

The north of me,
To the east
Of that center
The south
Of my wandering
And into the
West of thoughts.
Waiting for words,
Limbo of us.

Podunk Moon

A flat tire wasn't
Just a possibility
You could call it
A sure thing.
It was like
The surface
Of the moon,
The Podunk town
Didn't care,
Their pockets
Had been sewn shut
Years ago. Years before
This haunted June
Had come and taken
So many
That the graveyard
Was overrun with
Shoeprints, and
Tiny holes made by
Low rent heels.
There was hardly
Anyone left to bury
The ones that kept
Dying and they didn't
Just die once,

They died over
And over again
As if they enjoyed
The funeral procedure,
And again
The mourners cried,
Because they had nothing
Better to do
And nowhere
Else to go.

Erin Geil, author of Podunk Moon, has been published in the Calliope Journal at West Virginia University, and has had a piece of flash fiction published in, Diner Stories: Off the Menu. She lives out most of her days surrounded by cats. And can be reached at authoreringeil via Instagram.

Mark Husk

Poetry Will Come
(published on newmystics.com)

I must wait for Poetry to come
and I know that it will
but in its own good time,
and in its own silent way.

And it will whisper what I need to know
about life and death
hope and pain
and redemption through it all.

But I must be patient and very still
for Poetry has its own quiet Way,
its very own Heart,
and its own subtle Stories to tell.

And it cannot be heard
over the din and crash of this hectic life.
the constant conflict in my mind
and the chaos of the world around.

So I will sit here quietly
and listen very carefully,
and someday perhaps I can tell to you
the Stories that Poetry has for me.

He Knows That She Knows
(Published on Newmystics.com)

He helps her put on her coat,
and he smiles.
He's done this for fifty-three years now,
and he doesn't mind at all,
because he knows that she knows.

He hands her the walking cane,
something he's had to do more recently,
but he smiles, and doesn't mind at all
because he knows that she knows.

And her purse he carries with him
as they make their shuffling way towards the door,
and still he smiles, and doesn't mind at all,
because he knows that she knows.

And he knows that fifty-three years
is a long time to spend with someone else,
unless it's with someone you love
and then it's not so long at all.

Miles To Go

His feet have seen a lot of miles over the years.

1938
Ten years old and running
barefoot through the grass,
over hills and across fields in the evenings of summer,
chasing cattle towards the barn
out of breath but happy,
anticipating the shiny nickel
his grandfather had for him when he got back.

1942
Skipping over slimy rocks,
balancing as he crosses a fallen log,
a short hike to the dipping hole,
and the bloody hobble back home,
long and painful,
with a fresh cut from a piece of broken ceramic
half buried and hidden
in the depths of the water.

1952
Blisters on top of blisters,
soaking wet for days,
the heat and cold,
the rain and the pain

of South Korea,
the weight of the pack getting heavier
mile after mile,
and day after day.

1954
Shiny dress shoes,
pinching and much too tight,
as he tries to stand perfectly still
waiting for his beautiful bride,
that all-too-quick walk back down the aisle,
and those stumbling awkward steps,
of that very first dance,
one of many
with his brand new wife.

1956
A hurried half-sprint in bedroom slippers,
out the front door and into the car,
trying to remember everything he is supposed to bring,
and praying,
praying,
praying
to get to the delivery room on time.

1978
And once again in shiny shoes much too tight,
and another slower walk down a holy aisle,

to give away his pride and joy
to a younger version of himself,
and watch as they too, stumble through their very
first dance.
He smiles then, a genuine smile,
and tight shoes be damned,
he takes his own bride by the hand,
and shows them how it's done.

1995
Grease and oil and gasoline
stain his old work shoes,
another pair almost worn out
a mechanic's job is hard on them
but he wouldn't trade it
for anything in the world.

2016
Now his work shoes are replaced by softer ones,
more comfortable,
easy to slip on and take off,
without having to bend over quite so much.

And with a little bit of help from his walking cane,
he makes his way down the hall to bed each night,
to sleep next to his favorite dance partner
for so many, many years.

And he prays.

He prays that even now,
near the end of the road,
he still has a few more miles left
and maybe one more dance.

I've Got Nothing To Do

I think what I need to do,
is to block some time in my schedule
to do Nothing.

Maybe just an hour or so
to watch the clouds go by,
or listen as the birds sing in the trees.
.

Some time for my lazy thoughts
to wander where they will,
and to rest my soul a bit.

I'll have to write it on my calendar I'm afraid,
so that Something doesn't come up
and interfere with my plan to do Nothing.

Because I have a lot of Nothing that needs to get done..
It's piled up and well overdue,
and I need to get started on it.
.

I Shall Go Back

I shall go back
to the wooded mountains
and dark forest paths
that knows my name well
and I know theirs.

To rocky tumbling streams
and lazy clouds making their way
across the clear blue sky
whispering their greetings
in the wind.

To visit for a while the giant trees
full of strength and memory
and spend some lonely time
resting in their shade
and remembering

that the grass and rocks and dirt
under my tired and wandering feet
has always been
and will always be
waiting patiently
for my return.

I shall go back.

Mark was born and raised in the hills of West Virginia. His poetry and musings have been published at Newmystics.com, Art4theHomeless webzine, and in Whetstone, the literary journal of Fairmont State University where he won an Award of Excellence for his poetry. He is also the author of "Not So Common Sense: a little book of reminders for those in early recovery". When he's not writing, he works as an addictions therapist in Fairmont, where he lives with his cat, his books, his hiking boots, and his favorite cast iron skillet.

Kirk Judd

Chop Wood
For Rebecca

Remember, the ax must be sharp
Otherwise, the work is harder,
But chopping wood is chopping wood,
Not thinking about chopping wood,
Or writing about it,
Or singing it or telling its story.
It is doing work.

And when you do work
The words fall out in a line,
Make a path to follow
And you do.

More wood, more words,
And soon you are down
That path, deep
In that beautiful/terrible place
The work
Has taken you.

Chop wood means chop wood,

But it can and will take you
Anywhere you want
Or don't want
To go.

Year

June

    a waterfall in the road

July

    fireworks on the farm
    a water truck stands ready
    slick from birth,
    a great-grandson comes

August

    a second cutting of hay
    sweat like water rolls down my back

September

    the river is dry
    turtles mud up in the pond

October

    rain collects
in the bottoms
of candy bags and jack-o-lanterns

November

    on the table
water glasses sparkle under candles
family smiles,
asks for pie

December

    before the tree dries out,
fill the stand
pine needles in the rug

January

    fireworks now are cold
stars shine like water
droplets in the sky

February

    ice

March

    muddy roads
    and green
    hints it is coming

April

    peepers are happy
    and let you know it
    everything wet

May

    trout fishing
    grass cutting
    bass in the pond
    leap
    geese and goslings swim

The Poetry of Trees

This is the way they write,
With blossom, and bloom,
And the beginnings of green.

When you see them, you know
You are hearing poetry
Hearing words you no longer understand
Hearing the sound of color

When you send your children
To the top of the hill to look,
When you send your grandchildren
And their children and grandchildren
To the top of the hill behind the barn
To look down across the meadow
And the small pond,
When you send them to the top
Of the hill in April
To look down at the edge of the wood
There past the small pond
And the meadow
To see the poetry of the redbud in bloom,
The clouds of purple
Whispering in that old language
This elegy to this Spring,
Whispering, those purple clouds

In that old language, the poetry
Those children will hear,
Will recognize, will never forget…

When you send them,
Tell them this,
Tell them I said to them,
Say to them now,
"I planted these for you".

Human Beings are Crazy and It Is Getting Worse

But
there are flowering crab-apple trees
and dogwoods
and azaleas
and just now,
a kestrel on the fence row…

When I listen, I hear them.
whisper,
"Pay attention.
 Be patient.
 We are here.

 You are not so old,
 or so different,
 and everything,
 everything
 takes time."

Kirk Judd has lived, worked, trout fished and wandered around in West Virginia all of his life. Kirk was a member of the Appalachian Literary League, a founding member and former president (and JUG recipient) of West Virginia Writers, Inc. , and is a founding member of and creative writing instructor for Allegheny Echoes, Inc., dedicated to the support and preservation of WV cultural heritage arts. Author of 3 collections of poetry *"Field of Vision"* 1986, *"Tao-Billy"* 1996, and *"My People Was Music"* 2014, and a co-editor of the highly acclaimed anthology, *"Wild, Sweet Notes – 50 Years of West Virginia Poetry 1950 – 1999"*, he is widely published. He is internationally known for his performance work combining poetry and old time music, and has performed poetry in Ireland and across West Virginia at fairs, concerts, and festivals for the past 40 years.

Daniel McTaggart

High Street At Sunset

The sidewalks are all redone
No more bite-mark shadows
Stretching like black tape
Over cracks in momma's backs

Benches on Wall Street are gone
The homeless can now go back
To dying beneath abandoned awnings
Expiring in old, familiar alleys

One man sleeps in a doorway
The sun warming his belly
His bare, hairy midriff
Powdered by gravel and ash

There's still a few places to eat
Neon blinks like newborns' eyes
Asking where's the damn doctor
Who spanked me just now

I keep pulling on locked doors of
Places closed since high school

I have memories still inside
Eating better than I have in years

I'm asked over lunch when did we
Get so old and I said it had
To be when we graduated, it had
To be when we graduated

Every Step I Take

I want to make an impact on the world I want
Every footstep to explode every
Time I walk into future time

To feel mushroom clouds bloom up
Between my toes with the vertical
Exhaust of a dying patch of land

Fallout will fill my wake like snow
Out of season and deadly to any
Who dares to follow my path

I am amused at how annihilation takes
Forms like beautiful petals
Pyroclastic bonsais for trimming

In any case it's hard to trace
The roots of one's steps in any case
Survival and dying are opposing art forms

Coffee At Beaver's Restaurant

My wrist drifted to the section
Of the menu listing
Various orders of coffee

My lazy finger jabbed
Blindly with weight
Landing like a wet rag

"Black-no-sugar it is"
Said the wide-hipped waitress
As she swiped the menu

Her gait sent shimmers
Through mist rising
From midnight cigarettes

The cup landed with a clank
Filling the saucer
With a little brown moat

Curls off the waitress' wake
Mixing with ambient clatter
Of dishes and rockabilly twang

This poem published in a different form in "Diner Poems", 2009

Not Unattractive Yet

The waitress is still young
Her skin is still clear
Not showing pockmarks
From a three-pack-a-day habit

Male consumers still glance
At her cleavage every time
She leans over the counter
She's not unattractive yet

Even with handles on her hips
A slight pooch over her waistline
Or the winged tramp stamp
Revealed when she bends over

Her long brown hair is tied
In a short bob that flails
With every sweep of
Her slender neck

When she arches her back
Her butt still sticks out
Farther than her stomach
So she's not unattractive yet

This poem published in a different form in "Diner Poems" 2009

Waitress In The Batman Shirt

I told her she should have
A utility belt for bussing tables

She said it sure would help
But cargo pants would be better

Only problem is
They aren't made anymore

So thanks cargo pants company
Now she can't fight crime

This poem published in a different form in "Diner Poems" 2009

Daniel McTaggart's poetry has been published in Amomancies, Backbone Mountain Review, and Kestrel. Recently, he has appeared in "BE-AT: An Anthology of National & International Beat Poets Laureate" and the 5th Anniversary Edition of "Bards Against Hunger". He has published several books of poetry. Most notably "Midnight Muse in a Convenience Store", and "Diner Poems." On September 2, 2017, he was honored by the National Beat Poetry Foundation by being named the West Virginia State Beat Poet Laureate from 2017 to 2019. He loves to write in bookstores, eat in diners, and believes Jazz and the smell of coffee are the same thing.

Frances Van Scoy

My Favorite Day
written academic year 1957-1958

*This is my first published poem. It won a contest for
writing about your favorite day and was published in
my elementary school newspaper when I was in
fourth grade.*

Well, to start my speech I'll say,
"I don't have a happiest day."
I've been to Virginy
But not to New Guinea.
I take lots of pictures
Under light fixtures
With my father
Whom it doesn't bother
To take lots of pictures
Under light fixtures.

From morning at dawn
I have lots of fun
Save meeting a fawn
Til day is done.

Frost
written October 4, 1965

The demon frost is coming.
The signs of his approach are in the air.
My flowers will die if they are not covered.

I take old newspapers outside.
There are not enough newspapers to protect all of
my flowers.
I cover the largest plants, the ones with the most blooms.

But I'm sentimental.
I also cover some of the smallest, most delicate plants
In hopes of saving them for a few more days.

I'm angry.
Why do my beautiful flowers have to die?
I remember Jonah and the gourd and am ashamed.

1950
*from Diary of a Sexagenerian
written in June 2010*

*This poem based on my earliest memory is from a long
work of semi-autobiographical poems, written as if they
had been written at the time of events of the narrator's in
fancy into her sixties.*

Light and the tree outside the room
making moving shapes on the wall.
Familiar smells.
Her voice singing
 I'll give you some bread and some milk by and by.
 But perhaps you like custard, or maybe a tart.
 Then to either you're welcome, with all my heart.
The feel of cool sheets under me.

I roll over and reach for the thin wooden bars.
I pull myself up into a sitting position.
I stick my legs between the bars.
I look through the open door.
I want to go through that door.

I begin kicking the side of the crib.
I sing that siren song
 that always summons her.

Then she comes.
She picks me up
    and presses me against her breasts,
        those sources of food and comfort.
She carries me to another room
    and sits down in a soft chair.
We sit there together for a long time,
    and I am content.

April 24, 1971

written in June 2010

48 lines

This is also from the unpublished Diary of a Sexagenarian.
Something
    easy to describe,
    yet hard to describe,
happened today on a hillside outside Roanoke.

I sat on that hillside embraced by nature.
I saw the ripples on the lake below me.
I felt the warmth of the sun on my legs
    and the cool breeze of the lake on my face.
I saw tiny white spring flowers
    springing up through last year's brown oak leaves,
and I smelled the rich fertile smell of the natural compost
beneath the leaves.

I sat on that hillside
    embraced by creation.
I sat on that hillside
    embraced by creation's Creator
and I ached.

I sat on that hillside
and wept.

I wept because for the first time in my life

I KNEW that the Creator existed.

I knew that the Creator existed,
   not because my parents or the church insisted
     that I HAD to believe to be a good person.

I knew, and now know,
   that the Creator exists.

I knew, and now know,
   because the Creator's Spirit
     penetrated my skin
     and touched my spirit.

I wept because I knew
   I had not kept all of the Creator's rules.

I wept because I knew
   I could never live up to the Creator's demands.

And then suddenly I knew
   that at a certain time in history
     the Creator became for a time
       part of creation
       to change the Rules.

Now the Rules aren't what matters.
What matters is Relationship.

I longed for that Relationship
and in that instant knew
that I now HAVE that Relationship.

I knew and now know
    that I have this new Relationship with the Creator
    and am embraced by unconditional love.

My tears ended,
    and I was, and remain, filled with joy.

On Being Lost in Canonsburg, Pennsylvania, for 30 Minutes on September 13, 2017

The title of the haiku contains more words than does the poem itself!

Ralph Emerson said,
"Our notebooks impair our wit."
So does GPS.

Frances Lucretia Van Scoy was born in Ohio's Firelands region. She calls herself a semi-native of West Virginia because the families of her maternal grandparents have been in the South Branch Valley since the 1740's. She is a computer science faculty member at West Virginia University and especially enjoys teaching video game development. Her short story "Canning Beans" appeared in the West Virginia Writers' anthology *Fed from the Blade* published by Woodland Press.

Theodore Webb

The Keeper's family embrace the rising and setting sun.

Brothers and sisters drink from the misty tear ducts of
rivers.
Their arms shelter the caterpillar, deer, beaver and bear.
The eagle soars over the children's rocky backbones.
The oak sinks long curled fingers into timeless depths.

The Keeper of the Mountains built our home through
billions of stars, traveling through all forms.
The Keeper's fingertips know more than will ever
be known.
Longer still the Keeper whittled our land with the waters.

Softness transforms hardness.

Who will survive by destroying our brothers and sisters,
by turning one's back on the Keeper?

How are we stone to those things which softness loves?

Prophecy

Don't become your own self-fulfilling prophecy
Because you are the beloved, foremost
You're connected to others
It's true sometimes they don't see you
Remember, you're not seeing them
The blind shouldn't accuse the blind of darkness—
or silence
We're born—and reborn—to suffer
Forever building bridges with blood soaked nails
In spite of life there's love
In spite of death there's hope
What else?
The Great Spirit is a butterfly at the river's edge
On a never-ending journey to the other side

Sex is Just Another Word for Someone to Talk To

I want a lover who's not sexy—
Norma Jean, not Marilyn.
I don't want Hollywood sexy.
You can have hipster sexy.
Don't dare set literary sexy on my plate!
I won't lick okra, slimy.

Since sex is in sexy, let's talk about—

Sex

Let's talk about sex – how we're one big orgy of
consciousness.

How feminist is the idea of "sexy"? Can "sexy" be an
aspiration?

My period's complete.
I love men and women.
No, I don't believe women came from Adam's rib.

In men and women, we have critters aspiring to be gods.

I don't believe "sexy" will exist in the future.
Nor sex.

All that will exist in the future is Information

The god-machine

The God-Machine

The GOD-MACHINE

My lonely conversation with Itself

Joan

Joan raised an army of one.
Exponential poet, electromagnetic verse,
Rescue the dead from green paper.

Joan hugged the broke like resurrection embraces life.

"You are not who you think you are.

Would you enjoy a week when you don't plow money?
Seven days, you cultivate saints of literature.
Bloom with saints of science. Harvest saints of protest.

We become our atlas, where every inquisition teaches us.
Toast blood to the folks behind the counter.
Raise crystal to the half-divine:

'May I help you?'"

Help consume this. Vomit this.
Question this. Replace with:

"May I help us, all?"

Hear a miracle speak.
Green men burned Joan at the market—this bread,
breaking their fire.

Ripe

Alice and Neo grow tomatoes.
She plunges stakes—he builds cages.

Neo sprinkles faucet water on the vines.
Alice embraces rain—a shower, she imagines.
A THUNDERSTORM! Neo screams, welded jaw.

Be silent on foggy mornings, Alice.
Wait for Neo to finish hugging his Doberman.
Don't show Neo printed photographs of your family,
Alice.
Don't interfere with screen-time, decompression
from chores of flesh.

Tomatoes turn hues of blood.
Alice nicks herself with Neo's knives.
Stakes rot. Cages remain.

Theodore Webb was raised in central West Virginia and eastern Kentucky. Webb has performed poetry as spoken word in Fayetteville, North Carolina, Eugene, Oregon, Charleston, West Virginia, and Pittsburgh, Pennsylvania. Webb's poem, "America in Dreams" was published in Pine Mountain Sand & Gravel (2007) and his "Spirit Horse" was nominated for a Pushcart Prize after appearing in amomancies (2014). Webb is the author of the comedy stage play, "Zombie Texts from the Future" (2014), the novel, The STARLING Connection (2012), short stories, "Family Hour" and "Desperate Engine" (2008), available as e-books via Amazon.com and Smashwords.com.

Webb blogs at http://www.theodorewebb.com.

LIKE his author page at

http://www.facebook.com/theodorewebbauthor

and FOLLOW him on Twitter @theodoretedwebb.

Robert J. W.

Panic Attack

The entirety of my
flesh has become a
rapidly approaching
asteroid on which all
of society has come
to rest.
I've dissected every
outcome with fingernails
caked in my
own blood and
have found a
million diseases in
each one.
The future is a
gaping maw from
which I continuously
step back in
fear of losing my
gangrenous limbs.
These pills I
swallow with a
gallon of

sweat just
blur the teeth into
an anesthetic mess.
Just run.

Jupiter

I've been running from
ghosts in which my
bones cage like
snipers.
I tripped over a
civilization of
laughing fetuses and
fell
straight to
Jupiter and I'm
falling still,
counting the
specks of
nothing as they
pass me by.
I don't lose
my breath, nor
do I explode, I just
let the fall
guide me as I
pick stardust from
my teeth.
Where I'm going, my
ghosts will
never catch me.

Only I can and
I'm holding my own
hand throughout
this journey;
stronger than
everything,
able to
withstand even
space itself.

Depression

I watched as
pythons replaced my
rib cage and
constricted the
hornet's nest within.
I've spent the past
few days in a
lynching of
cut phone lines tied
to origami trees, constructed
from unanswered letters.
I see some
light enveloping me
but I'm not sure if it's
home or
a wild fire.
I don't care
either way.
Depression is
boring and
so am I.
Chemicals kill.

Even Eden Burns

She's scattered across a
thousand smoldering
meadows like
ashen rain.
All she wanted was
to grip their sunlight
in her hands but
her kindling skin
burned pink smoke that
choked out the
apathetic sky.
Their once lyrical
laughter now turns into
bloody coughing as
fire fills their
throats.
Is she beautiful
enough for them
now?
Is she a
harbinger of
sickness or is she a
tiny flower,
blooming into something
beautiful, only to

get infected with
the touch of
mediocrity and
Judas stones?

Dope Sick Children In Love

It will be
two years this
December since we
met and
collided like
dope sick children
in love.
I'm tired of
writing about it but
you bleed what
you know and
the cuts never
heal.
Our war of
mood disorders and
bad poetry left us
shivering outside
your apartment, smoking
overpriced cigarettes as we
wept into the
falling snow.
We would tear
the skin from
each other's bodies and
use it for

warmth, even when
the sun rose,
with smiles
branded on
both our teeth.
I still miss
the destruction of
our affair.
I can't even
recreate it by
having other girls
rip the clothespins you
gave me
from my flesh because
it's just
not the same
without you
and your
nirvana voice
reminding me
of the
sepsis
I am.

Robert J. W. is a poet, author, photographer, and digital artist from Morgantown. He is the author of the poetry collections *Houses I've Died In* and *Screamo Lullabies*, as well as an editor for Untwine.Usa. He enjoys reading, listening to music, and gaming.

James P. Wagner (Ishwa) is an editor, publisher, award-winning fiction writer, essayist, performance poet, and alum twice over (BA & MALS) of Dowling College. He is the publisher for Local Gems Poetry Press and the Senior Founder and President of the Bards Initiative, a Long Island based non-profit dedicated to using poetry for social improvement. He has been on the advisory boards for the Nassau County Poet Laureate Society and the Walt Whitman Birthplace Association. James also helped with the Dowling College Writing Conference. His poetry is also used for autism advocacy, having appeared at the Naturally Autistic Conference in Vancouver and in Naturally Autistic Magazine, as well as his essays. James believes poetry is alive and well and thoroughly enjoys being a part of poetic culture. His most recent collection of poetry is *Ten Year Reunion*. He frequently lectures on poetic topics. He was recently named the National Beat Poet Laureate of Long Island, NY. He has edited or co-edited over 50 anthologies.

Local Gems Poetry Press is a small Long Island based poetry press dedicated to spreading poetry through performance and the written word. Local Gems believes that poetry is the voice of the people, and as the sister organization of the Bards Initiative, believes that poetry can be used to make a difference.

Local Gems has published over 100 titles.

www.localgemspoetrypress.com

Made in the USA
Middletown, DE
15 October 2023